Around Grimsby

IN OLD PHOTOGRAPHS

CW00457259

The Bull Ring in 1910, with country carriers' carts parked ready for their return journeys.

Around Grimsby

IN OLD PHOTOGRAPHS

Collected by JANET TIERNEY

Budding
BOOKS

A Budding Book

First published in 1992 by Alan Sutton
Publishing Limited

This edition published in 1998 by Budding Books,
an imprint of Sutton Publishing Limited
Phoenix Mill · Thrupp · Stroud · Gloucestershire
GL5 2BU

A catalogue record for this book is available from
the British Library

ISBN 1-84015-027-0

Typesetting and origination by
Sutton Publishing Limited.
Printed in Great Britain by
WBC Limited, Bridgend, Mid-Glamorgan.

The bustle of turn-of-the-century Victoria Street, looking towards the Riverhead from the corner of West St Mary's Gate, marked by Charles France's fish shop.

Contents

Introduction

In the century spanned by the photographs in this book – roughly 1860–1960 – the communities of north-east Lincolnshire underwent some quite radical and dramatic changes. These were perhaps most visible in the towns, but were taking place equally, if perhaps more subtly, in the countryside.

During this period, the whole character of Grimsby, the largest settlement in the area, was radically altered. For most of its existence, the town had see-sawed between relative prosperity and near-terminal decay. It was rescued from the latter state by a speculatory railway company that saw an economic niche ripe for exploitation. The dock and railway combination initiated by the Manchester, Sheffield and Lincolnshire Railway must have succeeded beyond its directors' wildest imaginings. The development of the fishing industry, although helped on its way by a series of happy accidents, such as the discovery of rich new grounds on the Dogger Bank, would almost certainly not have happened without the massive capital investments made in the port from the 1830s onwards by the railway companies.

This was equally true of Immingham. In 1901 it was a small, insignificant village 1½ miles from the Humber, with a population of only 241, but the geographical accident of a deep-water channel in the Humber and the desire of the Great Central Railway Company to expand its successful operations at Grimsby led to the dramatic development from agrarian community to industrial port within a span of less than twenty years.

Cleethorpes similarly was a child of the railway age. In 1842 White's *Lincolnshire Directory* described the township as 'a pleasant fishing village and bathing place . . . allowed to be one of the most eligible and salubrious bathing places in Lincolnshire'. The impression is of a small fishing community gently evolving into a genteel watering place for the upper middle classes. By 1861, however, after the railway had reached Grimsby, it was 'occasionally crowded with visitors brought by pleasure trains from the manufacturing districts'. The extension of the railway to Cleethorpes itself completed the process and confirmed it as South Yorkshire's favourite holiday destination for the masses, its former identity as a picturesque fishing village being lost almost completely.

Photographs of rural areas before the mechanization of farming almost inevitably give a superficial impression of timelessness, of the immutability of the agrarian way of life. As such, they can be profoundly misleading as social docu-

The Plough Inn at Binbrook, 1861.

ments. The late nineteenth century was the start of a period of profound social and economic change at least as great as was happening in the larger towns. Throughout the second half of the century villages were losing population, and after the collapse of corn prices in the 1870s the ensuing agricultural depression turned a drift into a haemorrhage. Interestingly, this was not a simple migration from the rural villages into the expanding towns of north Lincolnshire, such as Grimsby and Cleethorpes, or even to Lincoln, although this undoubtedly happened to a certain extent. Favourite destinations were the coalfields of Yorkshire, Nottinghamshire and Derbyshire (although not necessarily to seek employment in the mines) and emigration was a popular option. Increased educational opportunities were blamed for raising young people's awareness and expectations, causing discontent with the rural lot.

At the end of the nineteenth century there was still a very sharp distinction between town and country, with very different lifestyles followed by the inhabitants of each. The urban habit of shops had appeared in the largest villages, such as Binbrook and Tetney, early in the century, although many villages well into the twentieth century still relied on visits by the travelling cheapjack and the country carrier for many items. Enterprises tended to be small, and communities largely self-sufficient. In 1868, for example, the 242 inhabitants of Barnoldby-le-Beck could support a shoemaker, a 'shop-keeper and draper', and a carpenter and wheelwright. The latter would, apart from satisfying the village's furnishing and transport requirements, almost certainly double-up as painter and decorator, glazier and village odd-job man, as well as supplying coffins and acting as undertaker. As the twentieth century progressed, the distinction between town and country became far more blurred; communications improved, and the countryside became increasingly, with the mechanization of agriculture, a place to live, rather than a place to live and work.

Looking Back at Grimsby

Tramway repairs at Hainton Square, in about 1908. The electric trams, introduced in Grimsby in 1901, were very heavily used, and despite cheap fares (and a price war with the railway) regularly made a good profit for the Great Grimsby Street Tramways Company, which owned them until 1921.

St James' House, Bargate, in the 1870s. The home of Dr Charles Bartholomew Moody JP, Coroner for the Borough of Grimsby and District of Caistor, it subsequently became St James' Choir School.

The Bull Ring, a roughly triangular space between the Old Market Place and St James' church, which, until the early nineteenth century, was the site of the fish and pig markets. It existed until the 1960s.

Grimsby's Old Market Place in the early 1920s, looking towards the White Hart on the corner of Wellowgate.

Wellowgate, still with its cobbles, and St James' church, in the early 1950s.

Old Market Place, in about 1946.

St James' church, in about 1863, with both the town halls on the right of the picture, the small Georgian building in the foreground, the newly opened replacement overshadowing it.

John Dryden's boot and shoe repair shop on the corner of East St Mary's Gate and Osborne Street, in about 1922. John Dryden is standing to the left of the doorway, and his assistant, Sam Merriman, is on the right. The boy is Merriman's son.

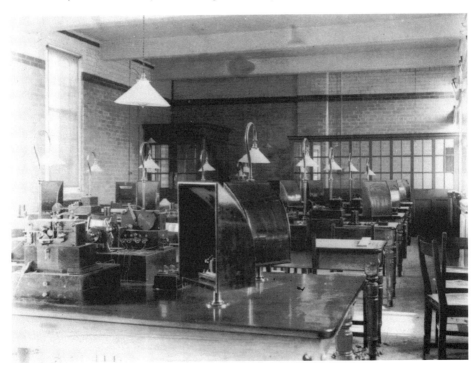

The instrument room at the new Victoria Street post office, in March 1910.

Little Edna Walsham stands in the doorway of Charles Walsham's confectionery shop at 183 Welholme Road, in about 1910. It was in the superlative location for a sweet shop: next-door-but-one to the Welholme Schools!

Eleanor Street at the corner with Hainton Square, beflagged to celebrate the coronation of George V in 1911. He was to visit Grimsby the following year.

The elegant and slightly intimidating frontage of Guy and Smith's premises at 19 and 21 Victoria Street, in 1920. The frontage has disappeared, but the building itself, extensively remodelled, remains as Binns department store.

Summer croquet on the lawn at Bennett Hall, in Eastgate, with the owner William Bennett and his two daughters, in about 1868. Bennett Hall had vanished completely by the end of the century, the elegant croquet lawn lying under what is now Pasture Street.

The Hull Banking Company's offices in Victoria Street in the last quarter of the nineteenth century. The building, largely unaltered (apart from the ground-floor façade), now houses the Yorkshire Electricity Board.

William Jabez Eden's stationery and book shop at 4 Victoria Street, in about 1880.

The Sime family had a long-established dyeing and cleaning business in Grimsby, the original premises in Victoria Street being operated by Alexander Sime at least as early as 1868. By the early 1920s, when this photograph was taken, the business had passed to Ion Sime, and new premises had been added in Cleethorpe Road.

The centre of late nineteenth-century Grimsby was ringed with cow-keepers and small-scale dairymen who supplied fresh milk to the townspeople. This is Isaiah Moyer's milk-house in Ainslie Street. The mill sails visible over the roof belong to the drainage mill at Ainslie Street cemetery.

The great Wesleyan Methodist chapel in George Street. Built in red and grey brick with stone dressings in 1847, it cost some £5,000, a vast sum when it is considered that the far more elaborate and only slightly smaller Baptist tabernacle in Victoria Street, built some thirty years later, cost a mere £3,500.

The Primitive Methodist chapel at Hainton Square, in 1880 before the road had been made up. The 'Prims', as they were called, were probably numerically the strongest of the dissenting sects in Grimsby, with seven chapels by 1905, including this one, built in 1873 with seating for about nine hundred worshippers.

Job Waldram, who rose through the ranks of the Borough police force as a sergeant and then superintendent to become Grimsby's first chief constable. He retired in 1892.

John Buttle of Scartho, at work in 1904 in the greenhouse at Solheim, Mr George Goddard's house on Bargate.

Grimsby Borough police massed outside the entrance to the former police station at the Town Hall in 1906.

A pre-First World War motorcycle rally parked outside Nun's Farm at Nun's Corner. The participants are well rugged, veiled and begoggled, ready to combat the elements and dusty roads.

Riby Square and Cleethorpe Road, in about 1905.

Freeman Street looking up towards Hainton Square, in about 1926.

The Theatre Royal in Victoria Street, designed by Joseph 'Nicnacks' Chapman of Freeman Street. The 1868 Directory mentioned that it would 'comfortably seat about 1,500 persons', but continued, rather ominously, 'it has been known to hold 2,000'.

Curry's Prince of Wales Theatre in Freeman Street, decked out with foliage and flags to celebrate either the coronation of Edward VII in 1902, or that of his son, George V, nine years later.

The Hippodrome Music Hall in Newmarket Street, in about 1910. Owned by the Grimsby & Cleethorpes Circus Company, it appears to have presented straight music hall entertainment in the early years of the century and then moved on to showing 'animated pictures', that is, films.

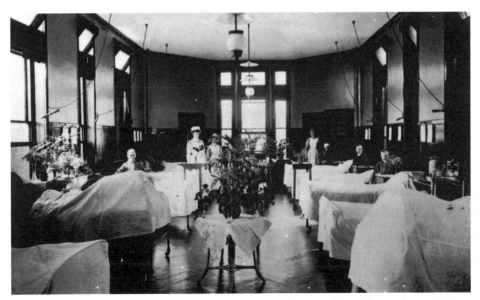

Yarborough Ward in the old Grimsby District Hospital at South Parade, in about 1910.

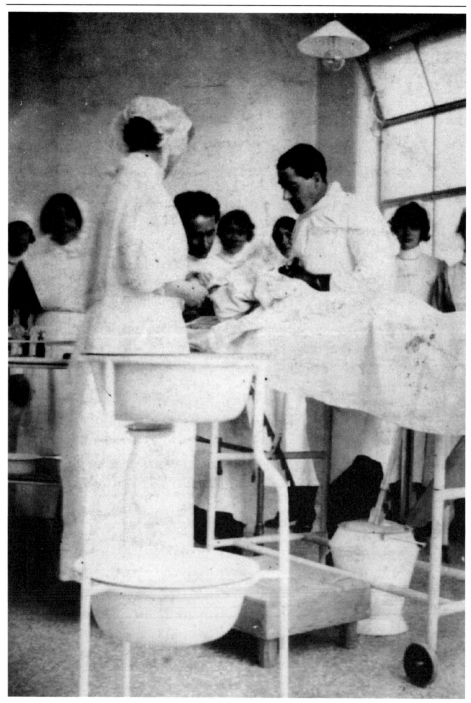

The operating theatre at Scartho Hospital, during the First World War.

Mr Robert Blow, gentleman, at the door of his house in Haven Street. The photograph is dated 26 July 1894.

Sir George Doughty MP, JP, standing proprietorially at the door of his home, Waltham Hall. Doughty, the MP for his birthplace, Grimsby, was an outstanding example of the poor-boy-made-good eulogized by the mid-Victorian writer Samuel Smiles. Born in grinding poverty in Robinson Street, he became one of Grimsby's foremost trawler owners.

A children's temperance parade crossing Hainton Square in June 1914. In the latter half of the nineteenth century there was a well-organized and generally successful attack on public and private drunkenness. There were many different temperance societies, but all had a policy of enlisting children before they could develop a taste for alcohol.

Before the First World War, the *Daily Mail* hired an intrepid 'aeroplanist' to tour the country in a series of publicity flights for the newspaper. The aeroplane landed near Love Lane Corner on 16 July 1912.

Grimsby Co-operative Society's organizing committee for their 1919 Peace Gala, and below, members of the sales staff pose in their splendid costumes.

Reginald Clough Mathews, pharmacist, outside his premises at 170 Hainton Avenue, on the corner with Catherine Street, in about 1930.

A spectacular fire at one of the warehouses at the side of the Royal Dock, 1914. The photograph was taken by a member of the staff of Louis Porri's News Bureau, ideally placed at 13 Cleethorpe Road for the scoop.

One of the pattern-making workshops at Harper Phillips' Albion Foundry in Eastgate,
December 1933.

An impressive display of carcasses on show at Robert Freeman's butcher's shop at 23 Oxford Street. The picture was taken in about 1930 by Stanley Warren.

A builder's gang in the Bull Ring, in about 1909, thought to be working on the premises later occupied by George Evington's drapery business.

Unloading beam sections on site for the Humber Street bridge in May 1932. The high-density terraced housing parallel to the railway line made tunnelling impracticable, so the traffic which the planned new fish dock was expected to generate had to be carried over the line instead.

After years of promises and hopes deferred, work finally began on the underpass beneath the Louth–Grimsby railway in May 1933. The photograph shows the work nearing completion, with the new railway bridge which replaced the narrow and hopelessly congested level crossing in place.

The new Corporation Bridge, opened in 1928. Behind it is the splendid complex of buildings which made up Marshall's flour mill on Victoria Street.

A Humber keel moored alongside the first Corporation Bridge, a swing-bridge of temperamental habits opened in 1873, and replaced with considerable relief just over fifty years later.

A grain barge drawing alongside William Marshall's Haven Mill at the Riverhead, in 1892.

The Riverhead in the 1930s, with a grain barge being unloaded at Sowerby's mill.

The Service Food Company manufactured pig food and poultry meal. This photograph, taken by local commercial photographer Joseph Bullen, shows its premises at Marshall's Wharf, off Victoria Street, in about 1937.

SECTION TWO
Cleethorpes

Cleethorpes pier, taken by a Lincoln photographer not long after it was opened in 1873.

Fishing smacks beached on the sands beyond the pier, photographed by William Garthwaite of Grimsby in about 1910.

Small fishing boats moored at Cleethorpes in the 1880s.

The first railway station in Cleethorpes was at the end of the Prince's Road, built in 1863 when the Manchester, Sheffield and Lincolnshire Railway extended its line from Grimsby. It was a fairly modest enterprise, as seen here, with a few buildings, a single low platform, and a turntable to turn locomotives round on the single track.

In July 1885, Queen Victoria's grandson, Prince Albert Victor, visited Cleethorpes and opened the Pier Gardens. To mark the occasion, Norwegian ice was used to construct a replica of London's Temple Bar, illuminated after dark for the two days that it survived by hundreds of gas jets.

A graphic illustration of the depredations of the sea at what is now the Kingsway, in 1902. This stretch of Seabank Road, as it was aptly called, was in real danger of disappearing into the sea.

The natural coastline of Cleethorpes was one of modest cliffs of soft boulder clay, which were being cut back towards the end of the nineteenth century at an alarming rate by the sea.

The sea defences before the building work on the Kingsway began in 1903 were primitive and fairly ineffectual; the soft clay cliffs were simply boarded up with planks of wood.

Blundell Street, as it was then known, looking towards the park gate. The bunting stretched across the street is in honour of the visit of Lady Henderson to open the Kingsway in 1906.

The camera was too far away, unfortunately, to allow us to see the golden shears which Lady Henderson is said to have used to cut the ribbon and declare the Kingsway – 'an esplanade second to none on the East Coast' – well and truly open.

Grimsby Road, in 1906.

Grimsby Road. This photograph was also taken in 1906.

The concert pavilion built at the end of the pier was a popular venue throughout the summer season. It was a pretty building, with its barley-sugar twist pillars and nautilus-shell-patterned ironwork. The photograph dates from the early 1880s.

The spectacular pier fire of 6 July 1903. Shortly after the orchestra had left, flames were noticed coming from the concert hall at the end of the pier, which was soon well ablaze.

A fine summer's day, 7 August 1911, and the holidaymakers are out in strength, making the most of the sunshine.

Sun-worshippers on the beach in the mid-1920s, waiting to be amused by one of the many beach entertainments put on during the summer season, judging by the orientation of their deckchairs.

The Figure-of-Eight Railway, one of the more enduring of the sometimes rather ephemeral amusements on the sea front, in about 1905.

The water-chute – a popular attraction in Edwardian Cleethorpes for only 2d. a turn!

One of the most enduring of seaside pleasures: boating, in about 1900.

Disappearing rapidly in the general direction of the pier is a sea-car, an amphibious form of novelty transport enormously popular all over Britain in the late 1920s. The sea-car's national debut was made in Cleethorpes.

One of the more curious amusements to be found at Cleethorpes was the Bicycle Railway, on which people could hurtle around a wooden monorail track, propelled by pedal power. All the evidence suggests that it did not really catch on.

Cleethorpes miniature railway (above) in the 1930s, and (below) with a few added refine-
ments and an up-to-date engine, in the 1950s.

Work in progress on the bathing pool at the southern end of Cleethorpes, which opened in the summer of 1923. It cost £32,000 to build, the workforce being largely unemployed men from the shipyards at Jarrow.

Cleethorpes was once famed throughout Yorkshire and beyond for its succulent oysters, which were dispatched to Hull, Leeds, York and Sheffield. But after a serious typhoid epidemic in 1903, the Cleethorpes oyster came under investigation, and the conclusion was drawn that the beds were probably contaminated by sewage discharged into the Humber.

The Cliff Hotel, on the corner of Sea View Street, and the Cliff Steps, in about 1930. Originally a private house, it opened for the sale of beer in 1863.

Yarra House in Alexandra Road, with copious decorations to celebrate one of Queen Victoria's two late nineteenth-century jubilees.

Maltby's grocery shop on the corner of Cambridge Street, a shop well known for good things, including a particularly distinctive blend of tea.

Cottages in Mill Place, in about 1900.

The splendid cast-iron drinking fountain, with its elaborate filigree dome, was presented to Cleethorpes by the Grant Thorold family in celebration of Queen Victoria's Diamond Jubilee in 1897. It was moved from its original location to a new site on the Kingsway opposite Brighton Street slipway, where it had to be demolished after a shooting brake collided with it in 1949.

The gas works at Beaconthorpe, built by a private gas company in 1864.

Cleethorpes market-place in 1900.

John Henry Kitchen's drapery business at 16–18 Sea View Street, with a fine selection of early Edwardian gentlemen's boaters in the window for cutting a sartorial dash in summer sunshine.

Cleethorpes, like its next-door neighbour Grimsby, owed its rapid development during the second half of the nineteenth century to the Manchester, Sheffield and Lincolnshire Railway. One of the outward signs of this burgeoning civic success was the building of a substantial town hall in 1904, at a cost of some £7,000.

The Primitive Methodist chapel in Mill Road was built in 1876 with seating for about eight hundred people; by 1905, this had become seriously inadequate for the congregation's needs, and an extension, with schools, had to be built.

The coronation of King George V and Queen Mary in 1911 was celebrated in style in Cleethorpes by a bonfire on the beach of suitably epic proportions, constructed by this enthusiastic troop of boy scouts.

Small fidgets at Barcroft infant school, in about 1900: not one of the children was able to keep *really* still for the camera as instructed, hence, no doubt, their teacher's harassed expression.

The Ports of Grimsby and Immingham

Peter Frederick Woldemar, skipper of the trawler *Emperor*, in about 1898. Woldemar, a Dane by birth, married a Grimsby woman and settled in the port. He is wearing a traditional fisherman's jersey, or 'gansey', wooden-soled clogs and thick woollen seaman's trousers, known as 'fearnoughts'.

Grimsby fishermen relaxing in port aboard the steam trawler *Renovo* during the First World War.

The crew of the steam trawler *Hawkins*, GY 93, in the 1920s.

Fishermen on the herring slip at Grimsby Docks, in about 1900.

Peter Woldemar's crew on the *Emperor*. The vessel was owned by the Anchor Steam Fishing Company of Grimsby.

Fishermen on the quayside at Grimsby, in about 1880.

The herring fishing was essentially seasonal, and the appearance of the shoals was increasingly unreliable as the twentieth century progressed. This photograph was taken in relatively prosperous times in the early 1900s.

The fruits of a trip by one of the Consolidated Trawlers vessels on the Pontoon at Grimsby in the early 1900s.

The crowded Pontoon at Grimsby, in the early 1920s. The photographer offered an interesting but temporary distraction to the serious business of buying and selling freshly landed fish.

James Carrick, skipper, in about 1880. The final photograph was to be tinted, and the photographer's notes are scribbled on the back of the picture. From these we learn that Carrick's hair was dark, his eyes blue and his complexion fair. His dress was black, enlivened only by a pale blue tie.

The steam trawler *Strephon* coaling in Grimsby's No. 2 fish dock in the 1930s.

Snow drifting along the North Wall and clinging to the masts of steam trawlers.

In the early 1880s, when this photograph was taken, there were no less than eleven ship-builders at work in Grimsby, and another two who specialized in the construction of iron ships. This fishing smack was built by George and Thomas Collinson, whose yard was in the Old Dock.

A filleting gang on the fish docks, in about 1910.

Laying planks on the quayside of the fish dock, in about 1920.

Charlton's was founded in 1862 by Thomas Charlton, originally as a shipbuilding yard. The firm was responsible for the building of many of Grimsby's earliest iron steam trawlers, although they were not concerned exclusively with trawler-building. After Thomas's death in 1903, the company concentrated on ship repairs instead.

The creature exciting such interest on a fish barrow on Grimsby Docks is a tunny, which had strayed from its more usual haunts in the Mediterranean. The photograph was taken in about 1930.

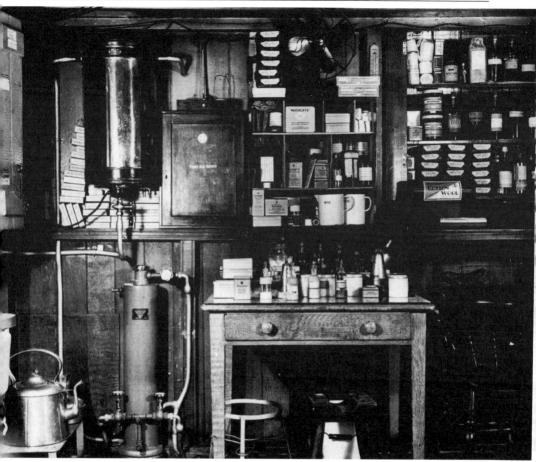

Known to workers on the pontoon as 'Charlie's', the first aid station at Cross Street, on the fish docks, was well equipped to deal efficiently with most accidents. The picture was taken in April 1938.

Unloading blocks of fish frozen at sea on to the dockside at Grimsby. The rather curious conveyor system was originally designed for unloading bananas.

Women and girls at work in the braiding rooms of the Great Grimsby Coal, Salt and Tanning Company, in about 1900. The demand for fishing net was such that an army of outworkers was employed in addition to the factory workforce.

Fish-processing at Ross Group, in about 1960. The photograph was one of a series commissioned by the company from commercial photographer Roland Burton.

Deal yard workers on the Alexandra Dock, in about 1908. Most of the men are wearing 'deal saddles' to protect their shoulders when carrying the timber. These were semi-circular pads of leather, stuffed with straw or horsehair and strapped across the wearer's chest.

Timber stacked in the deal yards around the Alexandra Dock, 1961. The photograph was taken by Roland Burton.

The ritual turning of the first sod of the Immingham Docks works in July 1906 was performed, with due pomp and spiritual guidance, by Lady Henderson, wife of Sir Alexander Henderson Bt, chairman of the Great Central Railway Company.

On 22 July 1912, King George V, standing on the upper deck of the Great Central Railway's newest Humber ferry, the *Killingholme*, pressed an electric button and opened the lock gates to officially open Immingham Dock.

The Grimsby & District Master Builders' Association, at Immingham Dock, September 1909. Back row, left to right: J.S. Fowler, Mr Garner, Wilfrid Wilkinson, Mr Redshaw, -?-, -?-, Mr & Mrs Seamer, -?-, -?-, -?-, -?-, -?-, G.H. Cross, Mrs Cross, G. Cross Jnr. Front row: Mr Hobson, -?-, W. Eglin, -?-, -?-, -?-, -?-, -?-, -?-, T. Frith Snr., -?-, Mr H. Cross, -?-. Staircase, top to bottom: -?-, -?-, -?-, Mr & Mrs Clark, -?-, John Gray, -?-, W.J. Cresswell, Mr & Mrs Robinson, Mr & Mrs Rushworth (President).

Official guests gathering for the ceremony marking the start of the Immingham Dock works in 1906.

The Immingham Dock lock gates under construction. At 56 ft 6 in high, and with each gate 53 ft 6 in in breadth, they were among the largest in the world when they were built.

Excavating the Lock Pit at Immingham. The completed pit was 1,000 ft long and 90 ft wide.

Immingham Docks, taken by Grimsby photographer Roland Burton in February 1952.

The engine sheds at Immingham Docks, in the early 1930s.

Unloading sulphur into lighters at Immingham. The photograph is one of the series taken by Roland Burton in about 1960.

Passengers disembarking from the White Star liner *Calgaric* on the Eastern jetty at Immingham in August 1930. The 'large and luxurious' liners of shipping companies such as Royal Mail, White Star and Orient used Immingham during the summer months for Scandinavian cruises.

Coaling at Immingham in the 1930s at two of the hoists on the coaling quay, which was on the south side of the dock basin.

Divers about to descend into the murk of Immingham Dock for routine inspections of the lock gates in the 1920s.

SECTION FOUR
Village Life

Only the arms of the signpost give a clue to the location of this photograph. The picture was taken from Barton Street at Laceby crossroads; the cottage has disappeared and the site is now occupied by a Little Chef restaurant.

St Helen's church, Barnoldby-le-Beck, in 1862. The church was restored in 1892, while its tower was rebuilt, at a cost of £1,000, by William Manby of Thorganby Hall in 1901.

The parish church of Old Clee, with its fine late Anglo-Saxon tower, between 1850 and 1860. The building was substantially restored during the 1870s, when a low lantern tower was added over the crossing among other works.

The Rectory at Barnoldby-le-Beck, in about 1862. The gentleman in the foreground is the Rector of Barnoldby, the Revd Morgan George Watkins MA.

Thomas Rannard, a prosperous farmer, stands at the front door of his home, the Manor House at Weelsby, in about 1860, with maid and groom in attendance.

The glorious Gothick pile of Bayons Manor, built by Charles Tennyson D'Eynecourt, a Norman baron *manqué*, in the mid-nineteenth century. Contemporary guides waxed lyrical about the minstrels' gallery, the 'numerous suits of armour, ancient weapons, banners and portraits'. Sadly, this marvellous architectural absurdity was levelled in the 1960s.

Swiss Cottage at Brocklesby in 1885, a Hansel-and-Gretel fantasy house on the Yarborough Estate, and a popular picnic destination from Grimsby.

The impressive Brigg Gate is the principal entrance to Brocklesby Park, and was erected as a memorial to Charles Anderson Worsley, 2nd Earl of Yarborough and Lord Lieutenant of Lincolnshire, who died in 1862.

The Mausoleum in Brocklesby Park was built as a monument to Sophia, wife of Charles Pelham of Brocklesby Hall, who died in 1786. The building consists of a chapel in the form of a classical Greek temple, with catacombs below.

Two views of the Temperance Hall in Laceby, both probably taken shortly after the building was completed in 1873.

St Mary's church, Binbrook, a 'small, plain structure', in 1861, seven years before its demolition and rebuilding.

The inn was generally the social centre for the village and surrounding areas. This is the Marquis of Granby kept by John Otter, one of two inns at Binbrook when this photograph was taken in 1861.

The quarterly meeting of the Duncombe Street Wesleyan circuit at Mr Simon's farmhouse at Tetney in 1914.

Wesleyan Methodists gathered expectantly at Humberstone to witness the foundation stone of their new chapel being laid. The original 1835 chapel, now the village hall, was outgrown by the congregation, and the new chapel and schoolroom was opened in 1907 on land given to the Wesleyans by Lord Carrington, the lord of the manor.

Binbrook formerly had two churches, St Mary's and St Gabriel's. The former was pulled down in 1868 and replaced by the present gothic structure on the same site. The couple in the picture, which looks to date from the late 1860s, are investigating the ruins of St Gabriel's, which fell down in 1822.

Four of the five bells of St Margaret's church, Laceby, in 1896.

Hatcliffe watermill and mill-house. The miller's wife, Mrs Harness, is standing at the gate.

Cottages near St Bartholomew's church at Keelby, at the turn of the century. The much-repaired exposed end wall of the terrace shows the original structure to be built of clunch, that is, locally quarried chalk, not the most durable of building materials.

Two views of the Louth navigation at Tetney Lock, where the canal passes through Tetney Haven into the Humber. The twelve-mile-long canal, which connects the rich agricultural area around Louth with the sea, was begun in 1763 and prospered until it succumbed to competition from the railways. By the turn of the century, traffic was reduced to small vessels carrying corn, coal, seed and manure between Louth, Hull and Yorkshire.

Island House in Pinfold Lane, Scartho, in about 1905. The house was continuously occupied for at least two hundred years by successive generations of the Kirman family.

Samuel Holgate's grocers and drapers store at Fulstow, in about 1905.

The interior of Will Phillips' grocery shop and sub-post office at Fulstow, in about 1910.

William Topliss's store at Ludgate, Waltham, in 1905. This was a fairly substantial undertaking, formerly run by William Topliss in partnership with his brother Samuel, with a branch at Laceby as well as a delivery service to smaller villages.

The staff of Barr's grocery store at Laceby, in about 1908. Top right, seated, is Charles Dickinson, while the man on the far right in front is Frank Allenby. The only female member of staff was Miss Stubbs.

One of Binbrook's several village stores, in about 1860.

A peaceful summer day at the turn of the century on what is now the rather busier A18 through the centre of Great Limber. The New Inn is on the right, and the village stores and post office, kept by Mrs Lucy Dann, is in the centre.

Kirkgate, Waltham, in the 1920s.

The clay lowlands of north Lincolnshire supported many small brickyards, producing not only bricks and roofing tiles, but also drainage tiles for soggy fields. This is Robert Harrison's yard at Fulstow, with Mr Mansell Richardson at work in the early 1920s.

Tetney Fair, 1910. The fair, fondly remembered by the oldest inhabitants of late Victorian Tetney as 'a period of universal feasting' (and no doubt a good deal of fun as well) had dwindled into near oblivion by the end of the century. It was revived in the early 1900s, but appears to have been very tame in comparison with its more rumbustious predecessor.

Frederick Broughton's Supply Stores at North Thoresby. Kelly's Directory described him, somewhat over-succinctly, as a 'grocer'. One suspects his own equally terse description of his shop is rather nearer the mark.

The smithy at East Halton, in about 1900.

Edwin Rimington, wheelwright, in his yard at Hatcliffe, in about 1920. Like many village craftsmen, particularly by the twentieth century when there was increasing competition from factory products, Rimington had a whole range of by-occupations, as an inspection of his shop doors reveals: joiner, paperhanger, glazier and perhaps not unexpectedly given his primary trade, undertaker.

Henry Freshney and his son Richard with the farm wagon built by them for Joseph Atkinson of Ludborough House, Scartho, in about 1905.

Henry and Richard Freshney at the entrance to their yard on Grimsby Road, Scartho.

Tommy Turner's smock mill at East Halton, in about 1908. Smock mills are tower mills built of timber rather than brick, and weather-boarded.

Colebrook's five-sailed tower mill at Scartho, in 1870.

Binbrook market-place. In the 1890s, when this photograph was taken, it was described as 'a thriving and well-built little town'; by 1930, its population had declined by over a third, and it was described, significantly, as merely 'a large village'.

Great Coates in the 1930s, photographed by Stanley Warren, and still a small and predominantly pastoral agricultural village.

Healing Wells Farm in 1932, part of the estate of the Honourable Gerald Portman, the lord of the manor of Healing. W.A. Thompson, a wagoner, is posed with Royal and Rattler.

Arthur Birkinshaw's wagon at Hatcliffe Top, in about 1930, driven by H. Webster. Dick Welsh is standing at the rear of the vehicle.

Thomas Charles (right) with some prospective purchases for his butchers shop at Arthur Kirk's farm at Scartho Top, in about 1922.

The Brocklesby Ox public house at Ulceby, kept in 1905 when this photograph was taken by Henry Jewitt. During the great period of agricultural improvements from the mid-eighteenth century onwards, particularly celebrated 'improved' fat cattle (and sheep) were exhibited around the countryside as an encouragement to farmers. Their names are often commemmorated in pub names; Brigg also has a Brocklesby Ox.

Lord Roberts, a fine Lincolnshire Longwool ram, being paraded around the auction ring at Caistor in July 1900. He was bred by grazier Henry Dudding of Riby Grange, on the outskirts of Grimsby, and was eventually sold for 260 guineas.

George Marris of Kirmington House, Kirmington, with his prize flock of Lincolnshire Longwools, in about 1905. The Lincolnshire breed survived the selective breeding practices of the eighteenth century which led to the demise of many of the old strains, primarily because it thrived on the lush pastures of the Lincolnshire lowlands.

The Laceby sheep-shearing gang at Keelby in 1907. The gangers, from left to right: Stephen Blow, Joe King, Tom Burley, Jack Best, George King, Mr Lowry, Ted Cross and George Drewery.

Sheep-dipping at Fulstow. The jovial-looking gentleman in the centre of the group has been tentatively identified as local famer George Pennell.

Harvesting at Binbrook Hall, September 1944.

Thatched haystacks at Great Limber, in about 1935.

The hay harvest at Humberstone; above, in about 1905, and below, with the aid of a steam traction engine, in the 1920s.

The Royal Mail cart at Binbrook, in about 1910.

The Tealby Express, with Mr Butters at the reins, in about 1905. The wagonette transported Tealby villagers to and from Market Rasen.

The post-mill at Tetney, operated by Henry Scrimshaw in 1890, when this photograph was taken.

Church Lane, Laceby, photographed in the late 1920s by Stanley John Warren, a professional photographer from Grimsby.

The Brocklesby Hunt's Meet in the Square at Laceby, in about 1908.

The cup that cheers: Huntsman Harvey helps himself to some welcome refreshment in the yard of the King's Head at Waltham, while the Earl of Yarborough's foxhounds mob a friend.

The Aga Khan Club in North Sea Land Humberstone, in 1922. Tom Hardy, the proprietor, and his wife Susan are seated, holding their two children, Frederick and Kathleen.

An election meeting at Laceby for the Grimsby seat. The Labour Party poster to the left of the door suggests this election may be that of 1892, when Henry Broadhurst, the Labour leader, stood unsuccessfully against the Liberal-Unionist, Edward Heneage.

Leonard Lond, the village postman at Aylesby, outside the post office hut.

Until the passing of the 1870 Education Act, which set up the first local authority run schools, primary education was largely provided by the British Schools, run by Nonconformists, and National Schools, administered by the Church of England. Waltham supported one of each.

Holidays in nineteenth- and early twentieth-century England tended to be few and far between, even for children, and the annual Sunday School treats arranged during the summer were eagerly anticipated. This is St Giles' church, in about 1920, in Pinfold Lane, Scartho. Sam Holdsworth, the headmaster, is in the wagon, while William Kirman holds the reins of the rear horse.

August 1914, and the (overwhelmingly female) members of the Waltham Band of Hope eagerly await their annual summer treat to Cleethorpes.

Immingham post office, in about 1920, in what became Hollingsworth Avenue.

Already acquiring nostalgia value as early as the 1920s, this mud-and-stud thatched cottage must have appeared impossibly quaint, rustic and obsolete to the new citizens of Immingham.

Humberville, Immingham, commonly known as 'Tin Town'. Described in 1905 as a 'small, scattered village', the start of building operations on the new dock in 1906 meant the rapid absorption by the community of an army of workmen. The prefabricated corrugated iron housing was originally conceived as a short-term answer to the housing crisis.

Immingham's new police station in about 1912. At the corner of Humberville Road and Pelham Avenue, it was built by a Mr Thompson of Scunthorpe.

'Humberside' or, rather, Humberville Road, was one of the earliest streets of 'permanent residences' to be laid out in Immingham, along with Spring Street (below), Waterworks Road and Battery Street. These rather dour terraces provided accommodation for some of the 2,000-odd workmen and their families, many of whom had migrated from Lancashire, the Midlands and Wales, after having finished previous contracts with the dock contractors, Messrs Price, Wills and Reeves of London.

Fresh fish from Grimsby. Mr W. Harris selling fish from his 'refrigerated bicycle' (a metal bicycle basket containing lumps of ice) at Immingham, in about 1932.

Healing Station in the late 1920s, photographed by Stanley Warren.

Ulceby Junction station and signal box in the early 1900s. The Manchester, Sheffield and Lincolnshire Railway Company, which built this branch line between Grimsby and Hull, was responsible for various grandiose projects in North Lincolnshire, notably investment in the docks at Grimsby and the resort of Cleethorpes. Returns were poor, and when these photographs were taken the Great Central Railway had taken over responsibility for this particular line.

The first motor-bus service in Britain was in Edinburgh in 1898, and motor transport was still an exciting novelty when this photograph was taken in 1906. The occasion was the inaugural journey of the Mail Motor Company's service across the Wolds between Caistor and Grimsby. This pioneering venture unfortunately collapsed the following year.

The successor to the short-lived Mail Motor Company: a Provincial Tramways motor bus at Laceby, shortly before the First World War. Provincial began running buses over the same route as the Mail in 1909.

Travelling to Grimsby on Mondays and Fridays, and to Louth on Wednesdays and Saturdays, Bob Cammack, the Hatcliffe carrier, was the vital link in the 1890s between the farmers of his village and their local markets.

James Westacott's removals van, parked in the square at Laceby in about 1930, with some of the contents of a client's house strapped to its roof and rear. Other road-users would probably be extremely grateful for its 12 m.p.h. speed restriction.

SECTION FIVE

People

Edward Jackson, known to
irreverent small boys as
'Jesus'. A shepherd and a
Methodist lay preacher, the
combination of this with
his habit of travelling on a
donkey proved irresistible.

Billy Gutteridge, the Waltham chimney sweep, relaxing with his pipe and little dog, in about 1930.

Matty Alwood, the Laceby chimney sweep. The photograph was taken in 1893 by Canon Henry Knight, the rector of Laceby.

Edward Abey, the keeper of Thornton Abbey, in 1850.

Monty Rimington, the village blacksmith of Hatcliffe, in the late 1930s.

The Revd Arthur Custance of Binbrook surrounded by a bevy of young Sunday School teachers, in 1905.

George Smith, the Laceby village schoolmaster, his wife and teachers, photographed by Canon Henry Knight in about 1893. The very youthful ladies would be pupil teachers, that is, apprentice teachers, generally bright ex-pupils.

While Parliament had accepted the principle of state provision of an old age pension in 1906, it was the so-called Peoples' Budget, introduced by the Liberal government of Lloyd George in April 1909, which made it a reality. Pictured here are some of the first recipients – those over 70 received 5s. per week – at Laceby post office.

John Kirkham, the first old age pensioner in Fulstow, in 1909.

Bobby Maples, the 'Laceby Hermit', poacher and gunsmith extraordinary. It was said of him that he had his annual wash on August Bank Holiday when he favoured Cleethorpes with a visit, and that his demise in 1927 was a direct consequence of the psychological trauma of being forcibly scrubbed clean in Scartho workhouse!

Horace Watson of Laceby, one-time postmaster, chemist and purveyor of Watson's Family Pills ('pronounced by numerous parties to be WORTH THEIR WEIGHT IN GOLD'). The photograph was taken by Canon Henry Knight in 1893.

Robert Harrison, photographer. The portrait is by Canon Henry Knight of Laceby.

Binbrook brass band, 1911, at South Elkington Sunday School anniversary. Back row, left to right: Harry Payne, Walter Firth, Edwin Briggs, Harry Plaskitt, Martin Scott, Jesse Bartoft. Middle row: Charlie Chapman, Arthur Dickinson, Fred Hall, -?-, -?-, Bill Fish. Front row: Harry Croft, Jeff Moncester, Teddy Harness.

Village brass bands were a popular form of entertainment in Victorian and Edwardian England and were often formed in association with temperance societies – even if temperance was fairly rapidly forgotten, band-playing being thirsty work! This is the Waltham Exelsior brass band, in about 1912.

A Thornton Curtis church group enjoying the summer sunshine in about 1910. The only member of the party so far identified is Mr Woods, standing in the centre at the back of the group.

Picnic in the sand dunes, probably at Sutton-on-Sea: the St John's church summer outing to the seaside, in about 1920.

Pupils at Wintringham Grammar School, in May 1953. Back row, left to right: Burton, Smith, Goddard, Evans, Jones, Jarvis, Cook, Stanley, -?-. Centre: Wressell, -?-, Smith, Evans, Stevens, -?-, Buck, Brumfield, Drayton, Pollard. Front: -?-, -?-, -?-, Ann Hopper, Mr Burnett, -?-, Janet Crowther, -?-, Sally Darnell.

Wintringham School girls' hockey team, 1922–3 season.

Members of the Old Winghams Hockey Club, all former pupils of Wintringham Grammar School.

Clee Grammar School's team for the 1902–3 season: Back, left to right: P. Leeson, Bert Buckley, B. Ingham, Willis. Centre: P. Woodliffe, Parker, Revd Mr Jones, N. Woodward, P. Cunliffe. Front: R. Blanchard, E. Buckley, E. Dodson, S. Dodson, B. Buckley.

The highly successful Welholme School football team of the 1918–19 season. Back, left to right: Dixon, Drury, Pacey. Centre: Denby, Swaby, Coombes. Front: -?-, -?-, Sergent, -?-, Winn.

Healing Cricket Club, in about 1905. Village cricket teams were generally speaking a product of late Victorian and Edwardian England, and their members were most likely to be shopkeepers, craftsmen and farmers rather than agricultural labourers, who were often too busy in the summer months to play.

Grimsby Amateurs Cricket Club in 1904: one of the four most consistently successful of the Grimsby and District clubs in the pre-First World War period.

The Fulstow cricket team in 1905. Will Phillips, son of John Phillips, the village post-master, is in the foreground.

An Edwardian tennis party at Laceby House, the home of William Field JP. Mr Field, looking slightly out of place in his town suit and bowler hat, is in the centre of the group.

The Revd Alfred Richings Tucker, rector of North Thoresby, with his family outside St Helen's church, in about 1910.

Fulstow Cycling Club on a leisurely trip through the lanes near the village before the First World War. A youthful Will Phillips, later keeper of the village store, is first bicycle from the left, sporting a handsome striped cap and matching tie.

Harry Thomas, one of the stalwarts of Grimsby Cyclists Club, with his safety bicycle, in about 1880. He had been the owner, until he sold it in 1879, of the first Ordinary ('penny farthing') bicycle in Grimsby.

Matt Brown, 'one of the most promising wheelmen Grimsby had ever produced'. The photograph was taken shortly before his death in 1896 at the tragically early age of 23, after he crashed into another cyclist during a race.

Arthur Bates, fish merchant and youngest
of three cycling brothers, in the 1890s.

Dennis Larmour, Grimsby Road Club
champion, 1932.

Pupils of Binbrook National School in the 1860s, carefully segregated, girls to the left and boys to the right, with the master, James Phillips, standing between them.

Young scholars and their teacher at Welholme Council School in Welholme Road, in 1905.

Children from the village school at Barnoldby-le-Beck with their teacher in the rectory garden, in about 1875. The school was built in 1862 by Richard Nainby, but by the 1880s it had closed, the children being sent to Waltham.

Pupils at Waltham Church of England School in 1894, with Robert Chiltern, the school-master.

South Parade School's May Queen of 1914 with assorted nymphs and bodyguard. Eva Dawes, with floral crown and sash, was that year's Queen.

May festivities at South Parade School in 1915. Some of the nymphs look less than enchanted at having themselves recorded for posterity in their spring-welcoming finery!

These four young ladies were participants in the decorated bicycle competition at Binbrook flower show in 1920. One cannot help feeling that Britannia's trident and shield must have made her forward progress extraordinarily difficult!

The Lord of Misrule and his court preparing for some jolly japes at a pageant in the highly appropriate setting of Bayons Manor at Tealby in 1939.

A trio of Grimsby boxers, in about 1900. Standing, left to right: Alf Wilson, S. Gray, C. Vicars, -?-, Mr Patterson. Seated: G. Wilson, Parker Jnr, S. Parker.

'Lord Street Prims' – the Lord Street Primitive Methodist football club in the 1922–3 season, photographed by Stanley Warren.

SECTION SIX
North-east Lincolnshire at War

Volunteers in camp at Thornton Abbey, June 1868.

Local Volunteers in camp at Brocklesby Park, in about 1898. They were mostly well-to-do farmers from the Brocklesby area. Standing, left to right: Richard Davy (Melton High Wood), Will Smith (Kirmington). Seated: John Davey (Goxhill), H.M. Foster (Melton Ross), William Lowish (the Manor House, Barnetby) and Harry Cartwright (Kirmington).

Grimsby's Alexandra Dock was regularly visited by Royal Navy submarines in the years immediately before the First World War, as this photograph from 1908 indicates. The town was used as a submarine base in the ensuing conflict.

Royal Navy submarines in Grimsby's Alexandra Dock in 1909.

In 1906, work started amid great secrecy on a wireless telegraphy station at Waltham, which started operations in 1907. The original crew, which included three post office officials, was photographed shortly before the First World War.

Mrs Stephenson, the daughter of John Andrew of Humberstone, organized pillow-filling for the army at her father's farm, the Manor House, during the First World War. The soldiers belong to the Manchester Regiment, which was billeted on the village for much of the War.

George Race of Cleethorpes, then a private in the Lincolnshire Regiment, with his wife in about 1916. Race survived the First World War, despite being gassed, and continued to paint the delightful primitive portraits of steam fishing boats for which, belatedly, he has become nationally famous.

The carnage on the Western Front in the First World War concentrated official minds on the role of women, as the suffragettes had succeeded in making them do with only moderate success. Women were increasingly called upon to take over work previously regarded as male preserves. These bus conductresses were photographed in 1917.

'Hitler gets Britain's last warning'. Grim news displayed outside Thomas Longthorn's newsagents at 203 Grimsby Road, Cleethorpes, in September 1939.

A crocodile of Grimsby evacuees, clutching their gas masks, file down Cleethorpes Road at the outbreak of the Second World War.

Great Coates Home Guard unit in training, 1941.

Fulstow and Marshchapel Home Guard, at Fulstow in 1942.

Minesweeper crew from the Royal Naval Patrol Service base at Grimsby with members of the WRVS, who were responsible for providing them with the vast pile of vegetables.

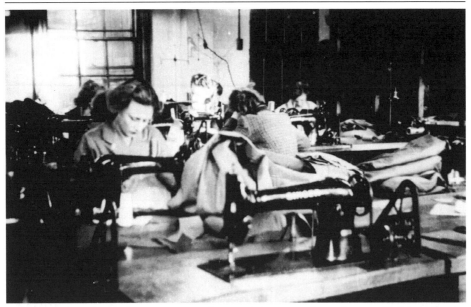

Women at the Pelwear factory in Grimsby's Dial Square making the so-called demob suits issued to servicemen on release from military service at the end of the Second World War.

The 'phoney war', which lasted for nearly a year after the start of the Second World War, provided an all-too-brief opportunity to train inexperienced civilians in civil defence, as seen here in a Grimsby street.

Old Market Place, Grimsby, taken in 1944, during the Salute the Soldier campaign.

Moving around after dark during the Second World War was a great problem because of the blackout. Hooded headlights (even for bicycles) were fitted, and the edges of mud-guards and running boards were painted white to make vehicles visible to other road users at ground level.

An ARP exercise in Grimsby in the early 1940s.

Flight and ground crew at Waltham airfield; the bomber, like 'Able Mabel' (below), belonged to the Royal Air Force's 100 Squadron.

Lancaster bomber 'Able Mabel' of 100 Squadron, based at RAF Waltham. 'Mabel' was one of only three bombers to top 100 operational flights with the squadron; in all she flew 121 'ops', 119 of which had apparently been completed when this photograph was taken.

St James' church was struck by a bomb on 13 July 1943 in the last air raid on Grimsby and Cleethorpes of the Second World War.

Still-smouldering rubble and a gaping hole mark the site of Lawson and Stockdale's Bon Marche store on Cleethorpe Road, destroyed on the night of 13 June 1943.

The children of Elliston Street, Cleethorpes, celebrate the end of the Second World War with a street party.

A Victory Tea for the village children at Waltham to celebrate VE Day.

Acknowledgements

I am grateful to the Director of Leisure and Economic Development, Great Grimsby Borough Council, for permission to use photographs in the collections of the Great Grimsby Museum and Heritage Service. The majority of the photographs are from the W.E.R. Hallgarth Collection, given to the Borough in 1979. I should also like to thank the following people, who have so generously made photographs included in this book available to the museum service over the past decade:

Mr Baker• Mrs Baker• Mrs Borrill• Mr Brevitt• Mr Canter• Mrs Charles
Mr Coates• Mrs Cooper• Mr Cusworth• Mr Davies• Mr Drury• Mr Farrow
Mrs Featherstone• Mr Ferrier• Mr Fitton• Mrs Fitton• Mrs Fletcher
Mrs Francis• Mrs Hancock• Mr Hepton• Mrs Horn• Mr Hudson• Mrs Jones
Mrs Lane• Mr Lidgard• Mr Lister• Mr Locke• Mrs Loftis• Mr Mackay
Mr Mashford• Mr Mercer• Miss Miller• Mrs Pike• Mrs Read• Mr Roberts
Mrs Smith• Mr Stevens• Mr Swann• Mr Taylor• Mrs Tuke• Miss Waldram
Mr Watson• Miss Wilson• Mr Woods • Mrs Worsley.

I thank also my friends and colleagues at Grimsby for their support and forbearance, and also my husband, who has tolerated much, and who can now reclaim the kitchen table for its proper purpose!